WHAT ARE AIR MASSES AND WEATHER FRONTS?

BOBI MARTIN

Britannica
Educational Publishing

IN ASSOCIATION WITH

Published in 2015 by Britannica Educational Publishing (a trademark of Encyclopædia Britannica, Inc.) in association with The Rosen Publishing Group, Inc.
29 East 21st Street, New York, NY 10010

Distributed exclusively by Rosen Publishing.
To see additional Britannica Educational Publishing titles, go to rosenpublishing.com.

First Edition

Britannica Educational Publishing
J. E. Luebering: Director, Core Reference Group
Mary Rose McCudden: Editor, Britannica Student Encyclopedia

Rosen Publishing
Hope Lourie Killcoyne: Executive Editor
Shalini Saxena: Editor
Nelson Sá: Art Director
Brian Garvey: Designer
Cindy Reiman: Photography Manager

Library of Congress Cataloging-in-Publication Data

Martin, Bobi.
What are air masses and weather fronts?/Bobi Martin.—First edition.
     pages cm—(Let's find out! Weather)
Includes bibliographical references and index.
Audience: 3-6.
ISBN 978-1-62275-787-9 (library bound) — ISBN 978-1-62275-788-6 (pbk.) —
ISBN 978-1-62275-789-3 (6-pack)
1. Air masses—Juvenile literature. 2. Fronts (Meteorology)—Juvenile literature. I. Title.
QC880.4.A5M37 2015
551.55'12—dc23

Manufactured in the United States of America

CONTENTS

LET'S TALK ABOUT THE WEATHER

People are always curious about the weather. We want to know if it will be warm or cold, sunny or rainy. This helps us decide what to wear. It also helps us plan what to do. Another reason we talk about the weather is because it is always changing. It can be sunny when we wake up but raining by lunchtime.

Weather can change quickly for many different reasons. But even when it does, you can be ready for it.

People who study the weather are called meteorologists. Some of the most important things meteorologists study are weather fronts. A weather front is the area between cold and warm bodies of air, called air masses. Watching weather fronts helps meteorologists forecast what the weather will be. And that helps people plan better.

Forecast means to predict the weather based on observations of weather conditions.

One of the things meteorologists do is watch developing storms. They gather information and warn people if the storm is becoming dangerous.

WHAT IS WEATHER?

Weather is a mix of five different features. The first feature is temperature, meaning how warm or cold it is outside. Wind, the movement of air on Earth, is the second feature. Next is humidity, the amount of moisture in the air. High humidity makes us feel wet and sticky. Dry air has low humidity.

The fourth feature of weather is precipitation. Rain, hail, sleet, and snow are types

Thermometers show how warm or cold it is. Hygrometers measure humidity. The instrument shown here combines both functions.

of precipitation. The final feature is atmospheric pressure. Atmospheric pressure is the weight of the air. Changes in atmospheric pressure help meteorologists predict weather. Falling pressure means rain is on the way. Rising pressure means nice weather is coming.

Snow can be dry or wet. Dry snow won't stick together to form a snowball. Wetter snow is perfect if you want to build a snowman.

Is It Weather or Climate?

Weather happens every day. But it is not the same in all places. The kind of weather found in an area over a long period of time is called its climate. By studying the climate of a place, scientists have an idea of how many sunny days it

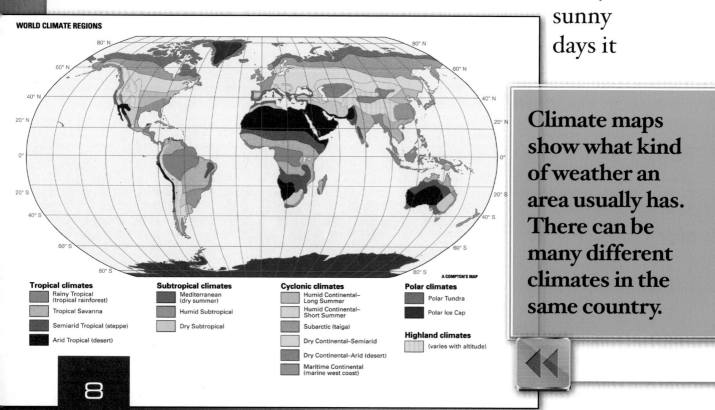

WORLD CLIMATE REGIONS

A COMPTON'S MAP

Tropical climates
- Rainy Tropical (tropical rainforest)
- Tropical Savanna
- Semiarid Tropical (steppe)
- Arid Tropical (desert)

Subtropical climates
- Mediterranean (dry summer)
- Humid Subtropical
- Dry Subtropical

Cyclonic climates
- Humid Continental–Long Summer
- Humid Continental–Short Summer
- Subarctic (taiga)
- Dry Continental–Semiarid
- Dry Continental–Arid (desert)
- Maritime Continental (marine west coast)

Polar climates
- Polar Tundra
- Polar Ice Cap

Highland climates
- (varies with altitude)

Climate maps show what kind of weather an area usually has. There can be many different climates in the same country.

Rice grows well in a hot, wet climate. But many plants, such as lettuce, celery, or peas, need cooler temperatures.

will have each year. They know how much rain it usually gets and if it might snow there.

Climate determines what kinds of plants can grow in a place and what kinds of animals can live there. Farmers use information about climate to decide which crops will do best in that area. Families use information about climates to decide where to live or to choose a good vacation spot.

COMPARE AND CONTRAST
Climate is based on weather. But how is climate different from weather?

AIR MASSES ON THE MOVE

Wind is always blowing somewhere on Earth. Wind moves huge air masses. An air mass is a large region of air that all has about the same temperature and humidity. Some air masses are so big they stretch across thousands of miles. An air mass can be hot or cold, wet or dry, depending on where it forms.

We can't see the wind, but we can see some things it moves. Wind can be a gentle breeze, or it can be strong enough to knock down trees.

A COMPTON'S MAP

An air mass that forms over land is a continental air mass. Continental air masses that form over northern Canada and over Siberia in Russia are very cold. If the air mass forms over land near the equator, it will be hot. No matter where it forms, a continental air mass is dry. These air masses do not bring much rain.

Continental describes something relating to or having the characteristics of a continent.

Maritime air masses bring warmth and humidity to tropical islands in the summer. They can also cause rain to fall over the ocean.

An air mass that develops over water is called a maritime air mass. These air masses have a lot of moisture. Maritime masses usually have milder temperatures than masses that form over land. Maritime air masses can be warm or cool. They will not be very hot or very cold.

The maritime masses that form over the North Atlantic or North Pacific Oceans are cool. Maritime air masses that form over the Gulf of Mexico or the Caribbean Sea are warmer. They often bring fog and low clouds when they move onto land. In spring and summer, these warmer air masses can cause heavy rains or even thunderstorms.

COMPARE AND CONTRAST

How are continental and maritime air masses similar? In what ways are they different?

When a warm maritime air mass blows over a cool surface, it causes fog to form.

Meet Me at the Front

Have you ever wondered what causes storms? Weather fronts are responsible for many kinds of storms. A weather front is the zone between two different air masses. Weather fronts can be hundreds of

Think About It

Understanding weather fronts can help us predict what kind of weather to expect. Why is this important to people?

miles
across.
The front may
bring big changes
in temperature and

humidity. The wind often shifts directions, too. These factors cause changes in the weather.

There are several types of weather fronts. Meteorologists know what type a front is by looking at two things. One is the direction that the colder air mass is moving. The second is what kind of air mass is replacing the other.

The red line with half circles shows a warm front that is moving east. The blue line with triangles shows that a cold front is following the warm front.

COLD FRONT

When a cold air mass moves into an area where a warm mass is, it creates a cold front. Cold fronts move faster than other fronts and can cause dangerous storms. Cold air is heavy. It forces the lighter, warmer air to rise. The warm air cools rapidly as it rises, and moisture in the air often turns into precipitation.

When a cold front forces warm air to rise quickly, the moisture in the air doesn't have time to evaporate. Instead, it turns into rain.

THINK ABOUT IT

Cold fronts bring rain in summer and snow in winter. Why do you think this is?

In summer this can cause heavy rain to fall or thunderstorms. In winter, a cold front can bring snowstorms. Usually, the storms pass quickly, leaving cooler, drier air and clear skies. Sometimes a group of thunderstorms form in a line, one after the other. This is called a squall line.

Cold fronts can bring snowstorms in winter. Snowstorms can drop several inches of snow in a short time.

WARM FRONT

Warm fronts move slower than cold fronts and spread out over a wider area. Because warm air is lighter than cold air, a warm air mass cannot push a cold air mass out of the way. Instead, the warm air mass slides over the top of the cold air mass.

THINK ABOUT IT

Storms in a warm front last longer than storms in a cold front. Why does this happen?

Most hail is small, but sometimes large balls of hail form. This hailstone is about the size of a golf ball!

18

When an ice storm coats trees, the weight of the ice can break branches. Sometimes it breaks tree trunks, too!

In summer, warm fronts usually bring slow, steady rain that lasts for days. Sometimes they cause thunderstorms or hail. In winter, a warm front might bring a mix of rain, snow, sleet, or freezing rain—or maybe all of those! If the air in the colder mass is at or below freezing temperatures, a warm front may even cause an ice storm!

STATIONARY FRONT

Sometimes when a cold mass and a warm mass meet, both masses stay right where they are. Because the two air masses are stuck in one spot, meteorologists call this a stationary front. One reason why a stationary front does not move is that winds from the two air masses blow in opposite directions. It is like a pushing match in which neither side wins.

A stationary front can sometimes bring rain. When the warm front has a lot of humidity, you might have to prepare for several rainy days.

If it rains too hard or for too long, the ground can't soak up all the water. This can cause an area to flood.

If both air masses have low humidity, then no precipitation will fall. But if there is a lot of humidity in the warm air mass, it can rain for many days. Sometimes this causes flooding. In the winter, a stationary front can bring dangerous ice storms.

OCCLUDED FRONT

Cold fronts move faster than warm fronts. When a fast-moving cold front catches up with a warm front, the result can be an occluded front. In this case, the warm air ahead of the cold front is pushed up away from the ground. The cold air then meets the other cold air mass that was ahead of the warm front. Occluded fronts often happen when two fronts circle a storm. In a cold occlusion, the air mass behind the cold front is colder than the cool air ahead of the front. The colder air plows under the cool air, pushing

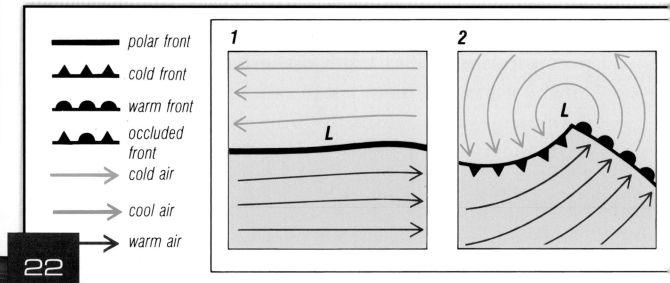

polar front
cold front
warm front
occluded front
cold air
cool air
warm air

When cold and warm fronts form around an area of low pressure, they pivot, or spin, like a cyclone.

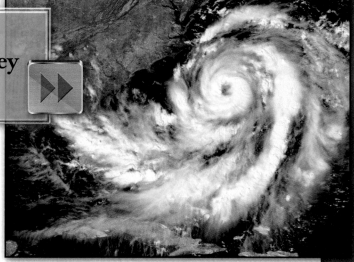

up the warm air in the middle and occluding it.

In a warm occlusion, the cool air behind the front is not as cold as the air ahead of it. The cool mass is lighter than the colder air. Cool air cannot push cold air out of the way, so it slides over it. As it moves, the cool air pushes the warm air up and occludes it from the ground.

Meteorologists use special symbols for each kind of front. Arrows show the direction the wind is blowing. The *L* stands for "low air pressure."

3

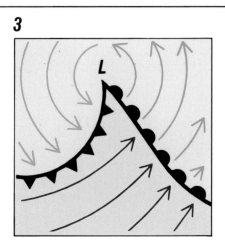

4

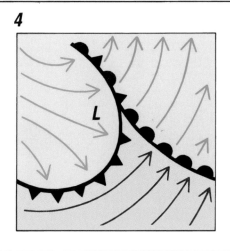

Jet Streams

You may have seen a meteorologist on TV talking about jet streams. These fast-moving wind currents move weather fronts. Jet streams can blow at speeds from 70 miles (113 km)

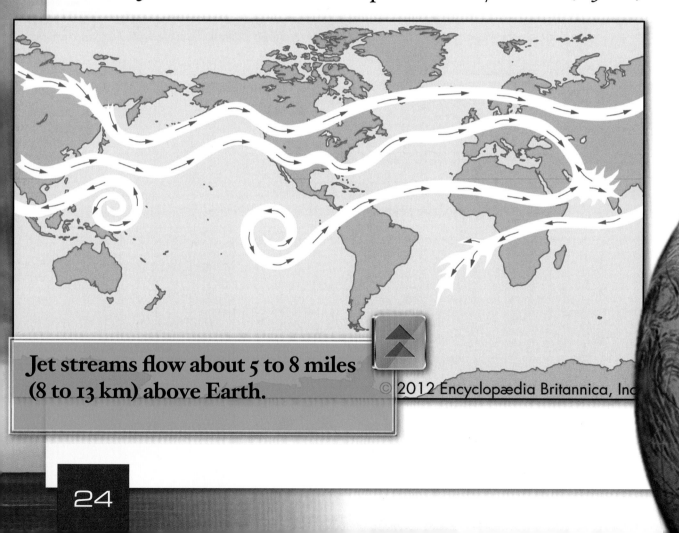

Jet streams flow about 5 to 8 miles (8 to 13 km) above Earth.

© 2012 Encyclopædia Britannica, Inc.

per hour up to 240 miles (386 km) per hour! They move faster in the winter and slower in the summer. We do not feel jet streams because they are miles above us.

There are two or three jet-stream systems in each hemisphere. The two systems that affect the United States are the polar front jet stream and the subtropical jet stream. Both jet streams move around Earth from west to east. They also move in a wavy north and south pattern that changes with the seasons.

THINK ABOUT IT

The polar jet stream moves lower into the United States during winter. Why do you think it is colder then?

Winds inside jet streams move at different speeds. The red areas show the fastest winds. The blue areas show the slowest winds.

When El Niño and La Niña Play

Every few years, a weather event called El Niño happens. The winds that blow across the South Pacific Ocean normally blow from east to west. However, El Niño causes these winds to slow down or even to reverse

El Niño can bring so much rain that certain areas may flood. Sandbags can help soak up floodwaters.

La Niña can mean that rain doesn't fall for a long period of time. This causes streams and lakes to dry up, leaving the earth cracked and bare.

direction. This makes the water off the western coast of South America warmer than usual. This causes big changes in weather patterns everywhere! Some areas get too much rain. Other areas don't get enough rain.

A La Niña event often follows an El Niño. The winds that get weaker during an El Niño become much stronger during a La Niña. This makes the water unusually cold from the eastern to the central Pacific. During a La Niña, the southeastern part of the United States has a warmer, drier winter than usual. However, the northwestern states are colder and wetter.

PREDICTING CHANGES IN THE WEATHER

Our weather changes from day to day. It can be hot one day and stormy the next. The weather also changes with each season. North America has warmer temperatures in summer and colder weather in winter. But sometimes events like an El Niño change the normal

Different seasons usually bring different kinds of weather. We can plan to relax in the pool in the summer because we know it will be warm.

THINK ABOUT IT

Meteorologists have an important job. What are some ways they help us?

Meteorologists must keep track of a lot of information. When weather changes suddenly, they're usually the first to know.

weather pattern. With all these changes, how can a person make plans?

Meteorologists watch jet streams, air masses, and weather fronts. They notice changes in atmospheric pressure, temperature, and humidity. Then they make forecasts. These help us plan for bad weather so we can stay safe. They also help us plan for fun events, like an outdoor party. With forecasts, no matter what the weather will be, we'll be ready!

GLOSSARY

climate The weather usually found in an area over a very long period of time.

equator An imaginary circle around Earth that divides it into the Southern and Northern Hemispheres.

hail Precipitation in the shape of balls and made of ice and snow.

hemisphere One of the halves of Earth as divided by the equator.

humidity The moisture in the air.

jet streams Fast-moving air currents about 5 to 8 miles (10 to 14 km) above Earth.

maritime Of or relating to the ocean or sea.

meteorologist A person who studies weather.

precipitation Water falling from clouds as rain, hail, sleet, or snow.

predict To make a guess about something that will happen.

sleet Partly frozen rain.

squall line A group of storms lined up in a row.

stationary Not moving. Stuck in place.

subtropical Of or relating to the regions bordering the tropical zone.

temperature The measure of how hot or cold something is.

thunderstorm A storm with heavy rain, strong winds, lightning, and thunder.

FOR MORE INFORMATION

Books

Christie, Peter. *50 Climate Questions: A Blizzard of Blistering Facts.* Toronto, ON: Annick Press Ltd, 2012.

Furgang, Kathy. *National Geographic Kids Everything Weather: Facts, Photos, and Fun that Will Blow You Away.* Washington, DC: National Geographic, 2012.

Graf, Mike. *How Does a Cloud Become a Thunderstorm?* Chicago, IL: Raintree, 2010.

Snedeker, Joe. *The Everything Kids' Weather Book.* Avon, MA: Adams Media, 2012.

Taylor-Butler, Christine. *Meteorology: The Study of Weather.* New York, NY: Children's Press, 2012.

Wendorff, Anne. *Ice Storms.* Minneapolis, MN: Bellweather Media, Inc., 2009.

Websites

Because of the changing nature of Internet links, Rosen Publishing has developed an online list of websites related to the subject of this book. This site is updated regularly. Please use this link to access the list:

http://www.rosenlinks.com/LFO/Air

INDEX